Individual Book Report Forms

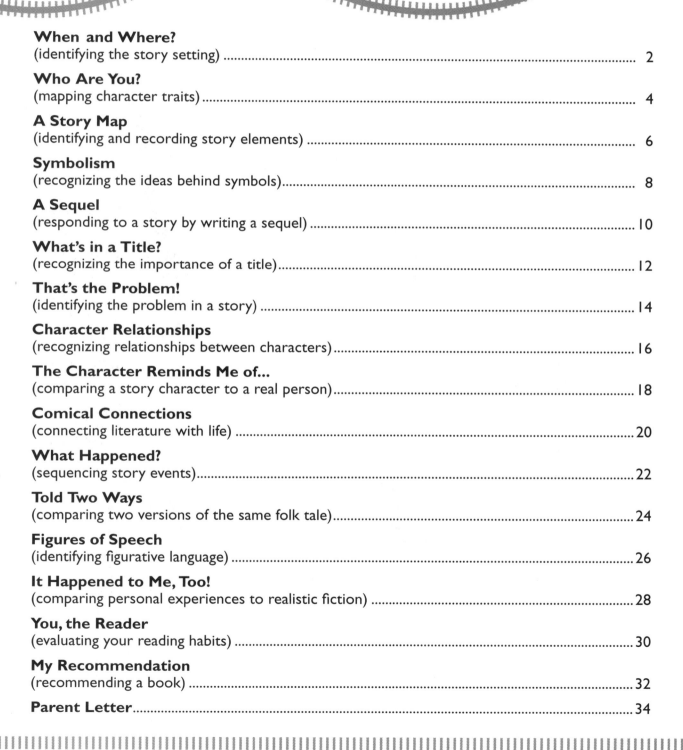

When and Where?

Individual Book Report Form

Literature Skill Focus: Identifying the story setting

1. Teaching the Literature Skill

- Review the term *setting* with your students. Remind them that the setting of a story is the time and place a story happens. Ask students to take notes on clues to the setting in the story you read to them.

- Read the first five pages of chapter I in *Roll of Thunder, Hear My Cry* by Mildred D. Taylor. On these pages, two brothers and a sister are walking to school for the first day of class.

- When you have finished reading, ask students to brainstorm the clues and then identify the time and place of the story. Some of the clues include "rusty Mississippi dust"; "bright August-like October morning"; "narrow, sun-splotched road wound like a lazy red serpent dividing the high forest bank of quiet, old trees on the left from the cotton field"; "Now it was 1933...." This story is set in rural Mississippi in 1933.

2. Reading Independently

- Have students choose a fiction book from the library. They take the book home to read independently. The students complete the form on page 3 and return it to school.

3. Sharing the Book Reports

- When the book reports have been returned, display them, have a class discussion about the literature skill in the students' books, or have partners share their books.

Good Books to Read

Fever 1793 by Laurie Halse Anderson

Johnny Tremain: A Novel for Old and Young by Esther Forbes

The Legend of Jimmy Spoon by Kristiana Gregory

The Librarian Who Measured the Earth by Kathryn Lasky

North Star to Freedom: The Story of the Underground Railroad by Gena K. Gorrell

A Proud Taste for Scarlet and Miniver by E. L. Konigsburg

Roll of Thunder, Hear My Cry by Mildred D. Taylor

The Shakespeare Stealer by Gary Blackwood

Tibet Through the Red Box by Peter Sis

Where am I?   What time is it?

Name_____

When and Where?
Individual Book Report Form

cotton fields...red dust...1933...Mississippi...August-like October morning

Title:		
Author:		Page Count:

Time	Clues to Setting	Place

Did the setting change during the story?   yes   no

If so, describe how it changed.

_____

_____

_____

_____

Who Are You?
Individual Book Report Form

Literature Skill Focus: Mapping character traits

1. Teaching the Literature Skill

- Introduce or review the term *personality trait*. A personality trait is a quality that describes a person or character. Some personality traits are *agreeable, curious, polite, friendly, shy,* etc.

- Read chapter 1 of *The True Confessions of Charlotte Doyle* by Avi. Avi tells the story of a thirteen-year-old girl caught between a mutinous crew and a dangerous captain on a transatlantic voyage. Ask students to take notes about Charlotte's personality traits as they listen.

- When you have finished reading the chapter, brainstorm Charlotte's personality traits. Using a transparency copy of the form on page 5, fill in a trait box and proofs of that trait. For example, Charlotte is polite. The proofs are: Charlotte curtsied to Mr. Gammage when they met; she called him "Sir."

2. Reading Independently

- Have students choose a fiction book from the library. They take the book home to read independently. The student completes the form on page 5 and returns it to school.

3. Sharing the Book Reports

- When the book reports have been returned, display them, have a class discussion about the literature skill in students' books, or have partners share their books.

"Charlotte dropped a curtsy. She called Mr. Gammage 'Sir.' I think she's polite."

Good Books to Read

Anne of Green Gables by L. M. Montgomery

The Bad Beginning by Lemony Snicket

Bud, Not Buddy by Christopher Paul Curtis

Casey at the Bat: A Ballad of the Republic, Sung in the Year 1888 by Ernest L. Thayer

Inkheart by Cornelia Funke

The True Confessions of Charlotte Doyle by Avi

The Young Man and the Sea by Rodman Philbrick

How to Report on Books • EMC 6010 • © Evan-Moor Corp.

Name_____

Who Are You?
Individual Book Report Form

A personality trait is a quality that describes a person or a character. Pick a character.
In the Proof boxes, write some things the character does that tell you who the character is.
Label each proof with a personality trait.

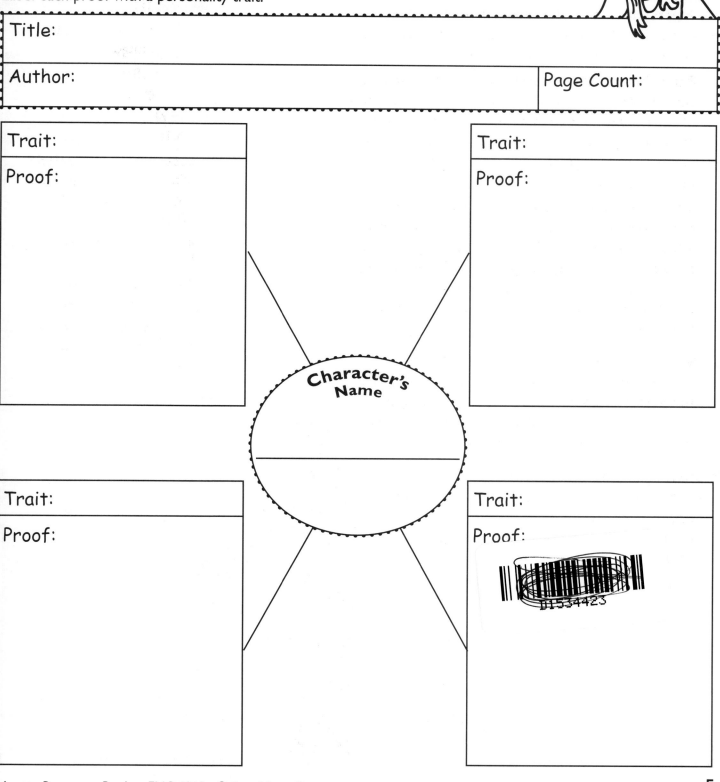

Title:

Author: Page Count:

Trait:

Proof:

Trait:

Proof:

Character's Name

Trait:

Proof:

Trait:

Proof:

A Story Map

Individual Book Report Form

Literature Skill Focus: Identifying and recording story elements

1. Teaching the Literature Skill

- Introduce or review the term *plot,* the action of the story. The series of events that make up the action is sometimes shown on a plotline. The plotline includes:

  the beginning, where setting, characters, and the problem are introduced;

  the middle, where the main character tries to solve his or her problem;

  the turning point, which is the most exciting or important part in the story;

  the solution, which is when the problem is solved; and

  the ending.

- Read a folk tale, such as *The Three Little Pigs* by Steven Kellogg. Model how to create the plotline.

  beginning: Mother Pig sends the three little pigs out into the world to build homes;

  middle: the first pig builds a house of straw and the house is blown down by the wolf, the second pig builds a house of twigs and the house is blown down by the wolf, the third pig builds a house of bricks;

  turning point: the wolf is unable to blow down the house and falls into a pot of boiling water when he goes down the chimney;

  solution: the wolf disappears into the woods

  ending: the three pigs live happily together in the brick house.

2. Reading Independently

- Have students choose a book from the library. They take the book home to read independently. The students complete the form on page 7 and return it to school.

3. Sharing the Book Reports

- When the book reports have been returned, display them, have a class discussion about the literature skill in the students' books, or have partners share their books.

Good Books to Read

Artemis Fowl by Eoin Colfer

Babe: The Gallant Pig by Dick King-Smith

The Borrowers by Mary Norton

Esperanza Rising by Pam Muñoz Ryan

The Indian in the Cupboard by Lynne Reid Banks

Island of the Blue Dolphins by Scott O'Dell

Lizzie Bright and the Buckminster Boy by Gary D. Schmidt

The Three Little Pigs by Steven Kellogg

The True Story of the 3 Little Pigs by A. Wolfe by Jon Scieszka

I told them bricks were the best!

Name_____

A Story Map
Individual Book Report Form

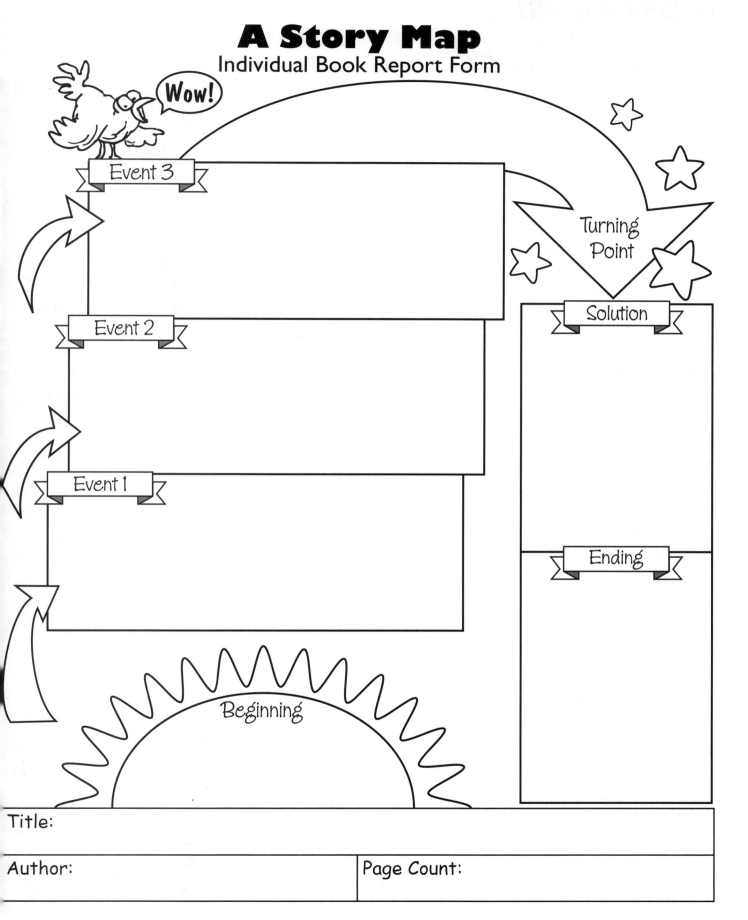

Wow!

Event 3

Turning Point

Event 2

Solution

Event 1

Ending

Beginning

Title:

Author:

Page Count:

Symbolism
Individual Book Report Form

Literature Skill Focus: Recognizing the ideas behind symbols

1. Teaching the Literature Skill

- Introduce or review the term *symbol*. A symbol is a concrete object that is used to stand for an idea. An author uses a symbol to stand for an important idea in the story.

- Read the picture book *The Wagon* by Tony Johnston. It is the story of a young slave boy's life and his longing to be free.

- Brainstorm the symbolic meaning of the wagon in the story. For example, the wagon is a symbol of freedom and the journey toward it. Ask students how the symbol helped tell the story. Students may also identify other symbols used in the story, such as the mules' names and President Lincoln chopping wood.

2. Reading Independently

- Have students choose a fiction book from the library. They take the book home to read independently. The students complete the form on page 9 and return it to school.

3. Sharing the Book Reports

- When the book reports have been returned, display them, have a class discussion about the literature skill in the students' books, or have partners share their books.

Good Books to Read

The Dark Is Rising by Susan Cooper

In the Year of the Boar and Jackie Robinson by Bette Bao Lord

One Candle by Eve Bunting

The Patchwork Quilt by Valerie Flournoy

The Tiger Rising by Kate DiCamillo

The Wagon by Tony Johnston

Walk Two Moons by Sharon Creech

A Wrinkle in Time by Madeleine L'Engle

What does the wagon symbolize?

Symbolism
Individual Book Report Form

A symbol is a concrete object that stands for an idea.

Title:	Author:
	Page Count:

Think about any symbols used in your book.

Symbols	What They Represent

Do you think the author's use of symbols helped tell the story?   yes   no

Give reasons to support your answer.

A Sequel

Individual Book Report Form

Literature Skill Focus: Responding to a story by writing a sequel

1. Teaching the Literature Skill

- Introduce the term *sequel*. Explain to students that a sequel begins where the previous story ends and tells what happens next. Usually the sequel has the same main characters and begins with some reference to the previous story.

- Discuss a book that all students have read. Ask questions such as:

  How did the story end?

  What do you think might happen now?

  What new problem might the main character face?

- Brainstorm an outline for a new story. Write the first paragraph that summarizes the action of the previous story and sets the scene for the new story.

2. Reading Independently

- Have students choose a fiction book from the library. They take the book home to read independently. The students complete the form on page 11 and return it to school.

3. Sharing the Book Reports

- When the book reports have been returned, display them, have a class discussion about the literature skill in the students' books, or have partners share their books.

Good Books to Read

The Cricket in Times Square by George Selden

Jumanji by Chris Van Allsburg

Letters from Rifka by Karen Hesse

The Snow Queen by Eileen Kernaghan

A Spree in Paree by Catherine Stock

The Twenty-One Balloons by William Pène du Bois

I like the Lemony Snicket books because the story goes on and on...

A Sequel
Individual Book Report Form
A sequel begins where the previous story ends and tells what happens next.

Title:	Author:
	Page Count:

If there were a sequel to this story, it might go like this:

Write the first paragraph for the sequel.

What's in a Title?

Individual Book Report Form

Literature Skill Focus: Recognizing the importance of a title

1. Teaching the Literature Skill

- Brainstorm with students why they think the title of a book is important. For example, a good title helps introduce the subject, sets the tone, and prepares readers for the interesting ideas that follow. Explain to students that often the title comes from a line in the book.

- Read chapter 1 of *The Egypt Game* by Zilpha Keatley Snyder. Have students listen for the title of the book as you read. Ask students what they think will happen in the story. Does the title help them make a prediction? If the title of the book were *A–Z Antiques* or *The Nosy Shopkeeper,* how would their predictions change?

2. Reading Independently

- Students choose a fiction book from the library. They take the book home to read independently. The students complete the form on page 13 and return it to school.

3. Sharing the Book Reports

- When the book reports have been returned, display them, have a class discussion about the literature skill in the students' books, or have partners share their books.

Good Books to Read

Al Capone Does My Shirts by Gennifer Choldenko

The Callender Papers by Cynthia Voigt

The Devil's Arithmetic by Jane Yolen

The Egypt Game by Zilpha Keatley Snyder

Five Children and It by E. Nesbit

From the Mixed-up Files of Mrs. Basil E. Frankweiler by E. L. Konigsburg

King of the Wind by Marguerite Henry

The Table Where Rich People Sit by Byrd Baylor

Tuck Everlasting by Natalie Babbitt

What's in a Title?
Individual Book Report Form

| Title: | Author: |
| | Page Count: |

What is the significance of the title of the book?

Do you think it is a good title?   yes   no
Why? Why not?

_____

_____

_____

_____

Think of an alternate title for the book.

That's the Problem!

Individual Book Report Form

Literature Skill Focus: Identifying the problem in a story

1. Teaching the Literature Skill

- Read the first chapter of *Hatchet* by Gary Paulsen. *Hatchet* is a story about a boy on his way to visit his father. When the plane in which he is flying crashes, he finds himself alone in the Canadian wilderness. He must rely on himself, with only the clothes on his back and a small hatchet to help him survive.

- As you read, ask students to listen for the main character and the character's problem.

- After students have identified Brian as the main character, ask them what Brian's problem is. For example, Brian is flying in a small plane above Canada. The pilot has just suffered a massive heart attack and seems to be dead. Students may also identify several problems in Brian's life that stem from his parents' divorce.

2. Reading Independently

- Have students choose a fiction book from the library. They take the book home to read independently. The students complete the form on page 15 and return it to school.

3. Sharing the Book Reports

- When the book reports have been returned, display them, have a class discussion about the literature skill in the students' books, or have partners share their books.

Good Books to Read

The Breadwinner by Deborah Ellis

The City of Ember by Jeanne DuPrau

Crispin: The Cross of Lead by Avi

Hatchet by Gary Paulsen

Number the Stars by Lois Lowry

Pathki Nana: Kootenai Girl Solves a Mystery by Kenneth Thomasma

The Shaman's Apprentice by Lynne Cherry and Mark J. Plotkin

Shiloh by Phyllis Reynolds Naylor

Oh great! Now what will I do?

Name_____

That's the Problem!

Individual Book Report Form

Every story has a main character with a problem.

Title:

Author: Page Count:

Main Character:

Describe the problem faced by the main character.

Tell how the problem was or was not solved.

Character Relationships
Individual Book Report Form

Literature Skill Focus: Recognizing relationships between characters

1. Teaching the Literature Skill

- Briefly review the term *character* with your students. Explain that a story usually reveals the relationships between the characters. Brainstorm and record possible relationships, such as friends, acquaintances, classmates, neighbors, and family members.

- Read the first chapter of *The Summer of the Swans* by Betsy Byars. The story tells about Sara and her relationships with her family members and friends. The relationships become clear to her when her mentally handicapped brother gets lost.

- Have students identify the characters and the relationships that are presented in the first chapter. The characters introduced in the first chapter are Sara Godfrey, her sister Wanda, her dog Boysie, and her little brother Charlie. Model how to write a few sentences about these relationships. For example, Wanda is older than Sara, and she has a boyfriend. Wanda seems impatient with Sara. Sara wants Boysie to play with her. Boysie is old and he sleeps all the time.

2. Reading Independently

- Have students choose a fiction book from the library. They take the book home to read independently. The students complete the form on page 17 and return it to school.

3. Sharing the Book Reports

- When the book reports have been returned, display them, have a class discussion about the literature skill in the students' books, or have partners share their books.

Good Books to Read

The BFG by Roald Dahl

Flipped by Wendelin Van Draanen

Harry Potter and the Sorcerer's Stone by J. K. Rowling

Jacob Have I Loved by Katherine Paterson

Kira-Kira by Cynthia Kadohata

The Lion, the Witch and the Wardrobe by C. S. Lewis

The Penderwicks by Jeanne Birdsall

The Summer of the Swans by Betsy Byars

The Whipping Boy by Sid Fleischman

We are best friends forever and ever!

Character Relationships
Individual Book Report Form

tle:

uthor: | Page Count:

scribe the two characters.

Two Important Characters

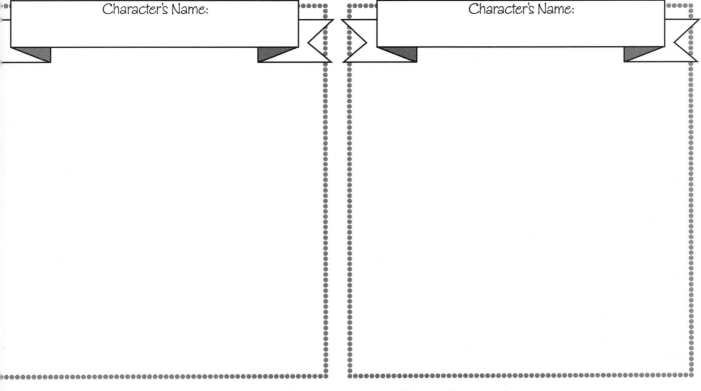

Character's Name:

Character's Name:

The Relationship Between the Two Characters

The Character Reminds Me of...

Individual Book Report Form

Literature Skill Focus: Comparing a story character to a real person

1. Teaching the Literature Skill

- Brainstorm with students the different kinds of things they learn about a character during a story: what he or she likes to do, how he or she feels, what the character looks like, and what motivates the character. List students' ideas on a chart or chalkboard.

- Then read chapter 1 of *The Rope Trick* by Lloyd Alexander. The story, set in Italy during the Middle Ages, tells about a young magician who wants to learn the rope trick, the greatest trick in the world. As the magician searches for the master magician who can teach her the trick, she meets many companions and learns to believe in herself.

- Using the ideas that you brainstormed, have students share what they learned about Lidi. Ask students if Lidi reminds them of anyone they know. Model how to write a comparison and support it with examples. For example, Lidi reminds me of my friend Lucas. She isn't afraid to stand in front of an audience. She loves watching the audience respond to her performance. When Lucas was the lead in the play, he was confident. His face lit up when the audience laughed at his jokes.

2. Reading Independently

- Have students choose a fiction book from the library. They take the book home to read independently. The students complete the form on page 19 and return it to school.

3. Sharing the Book Reports

- When the book reports have been returned, display them, have a class discussion about the literature skill in the students' books, or have partners share their books.

Good Books to Read

The Adventures of Tom Sawyer by Mark Twain

Bearstone by Will Hobbs

The Great Brain by John D. Fitzgerald

Hoot by Carl Hiaasen

The Little Prince by Antoine de Saint-Exupéry

Little Women by Louisa May Alcott

Love, Ruby Lavender by Deborah Wiles

Olive's Ocean by Kevin Henkes

The Princess Diaries by Meg Cabot

The Rope Trick by Lloyd Alexander

A Week in the Woods by Andrew Clements

You remind me of Harry Potter!

me_____

The Character Reminds Me of...
Individual Book Report Form

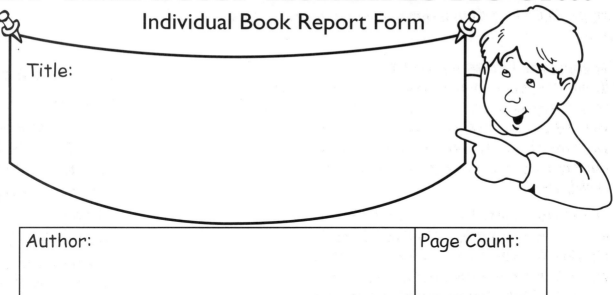

Title:

Author: | Page Count:

n Important Character:

/hat I Learned About the Character:

his Character Reminds Me of...
e sure to give several examples that support your comparison.

Comical Connections

Individual Book Report Form

Literature Skill Focus: Connecting literature with life

1. Teaching the Literature Skill

- Brainstorm the qualities that make a book humorous. List some characteristics of humorous stories. They might include humorous dialogue, comical characters, characters who are described in a comical way, laughable events, and crazy situations.

- Read the description of the Wormwood family in chapter 2 of Roald Dahl's book *Matilda*. Matilda is a brilliant five-year-old with parents who do not appreciate her intelligence. Roald Dahl uses sarcastic humor to describe the family. He is making fun of the Wormwoods. Ask students to describe a member of the Wormwood family or something one of the Wormwoods did. Then ask if that character or the character's behavior reminds them of anyone they know.

2. Reading Independently

- Have students choose a humorous book from the library. They take the book home to read independently. The students complete the form on page 21 and return it to school.

3. Sharing the Book Reports

- When the book reports have been returned, display them, have a class discussion about the literature skill in the students' books, or have partners share their books.

Good Books to Read

Everything on a Waffle by Polly Horvath

How to Eat Fried Worms by Thomas Rockwell

Matilda by Roald Dahl

The New Kid on the Block by Jack Prelutsky

The Phantom Tollbooth by Norton Juster

Surviving the Applewhites by Stephanie S. Tolan

The Teacher's Funeral: A Comedy in Three Parts by Richard Peck

The Van Gogh Cafe by Cynthia Rylant

Do you remember when?

Comical Connections
Individual Book Report Form

Title:

Author: Page Count:

When I read this book, the characters and events reminded me of people I know and things that have happened in my life.

Comical Character or Event	Connection to My Life

What Happened?
Individual Book Report Form

Literature Skill Focus: Sequencing story events

1. Teaching the Literature Skill

- Read chapters 1 and 2 of *Mr. Popper's Penguins* by Richard and Florence Atwater. As students listen, ask them to list the events in the two chapters. For example, Mr. Popper walks home from work. Mr. Popper reads a book about Antarctica. He tunes into a broadcast from Antarctica. Admiral Drake thanks Mr. Popper for his letter. Mr. Popper writes a letter to Admiral Drake.

- Introduce or review the idea of a timeline. Brainstorm how to put the events in chronological order. In this story, the order in which the events are revealed is not necessarily the order in which they occurred. Mr. Popper wrote the letter to Admiral Drake before any of the other events, but it was the last event described.

2. Reading Independently

- Have students choose a fiction book from the library. They take the book home to read independently. The students complete the form on page 23 and return it to school.

3. Sharing the Book Reports

- When the book reports have been returned, display them, have a class discussion about the literature skill in the students' books, or have partners share their books.

Good Books to Read

Aïda by Leontyne Price

The Birchbark House by Louise Erdrich

The Ink Drinker by Eric Sanvoisin

Mr. Popper's Penguins by Richard and Florence Atwater

Night of the Twisters by Ivy Ruckman

Princess Academy by Shannon Hale

Stuart Little by E. B. White

Top Secret by John Reynolds Gardiner

First, the sky got dark; next, the funnel cloud swept by; then, it picked up the house; and finally, she was off to see the Wizard.

Name_____

What Happened?
Individual Book Report Form

Title:	
Author:	Page Count:

Create a timeline for the book you read.

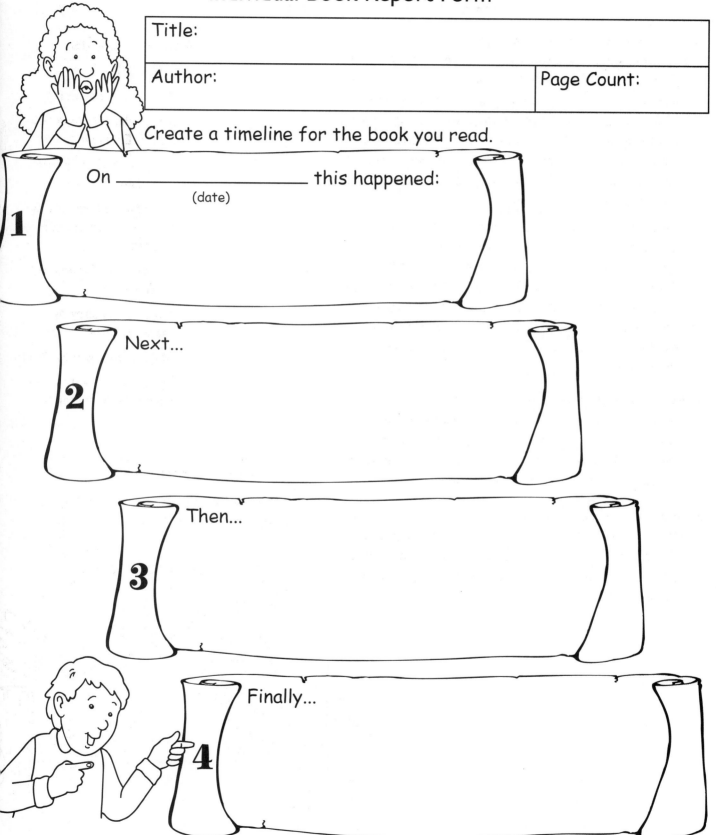

On _____ this happened:
(date)

1

Next...

2

Then...

3

Finally...

4

Told Two Ways
Individual Book Report Form

Literature Skill Focus: Comparing two versions of the same folk tale

1. Teaching the Literature Skill

- Briefly review the attributes of a folk tale. A folk tale is a story that was originally passed from generation to generation. Folk tale characters are usually all good or all bad and end up getting what they deserve.

- Read two versions of Cinderella, such as *The Egyptian Cinderella* by Shirley Climo and *Little Gold Star: A Spanish American Cinderella Tale* by Robert D. San Souci.

- On a chalkboard or an overhead transparency, reproduce the Venn diagram on page 25. Compare the two versions of Cinderella and complete the diagram. Finally, model how to write a paragraph that summarizes the similarities.

2. Reading Independently

- Have students choose two versions of the same folk tale from the library. They take the book home to read independently. The students complete the form on page 25 and return it to school.

3. Sharing the Book Reports

- When the book reports have been returned, display them, have a class discussion about the literature skill in the students' books, or have partners share their books.

Good Books to Read

Beauty and the Beast by Nancy Willard and *The Lady & the Lion* by Laurel Long and Jacqueline K. Ogburn

The Bunyans by Audrey Wood and *Ol' Paul the Mighty Logger* by Glen Rounds

The Egyptian Cinderella by Shirley Climo and *Little Gold Star: A Spanish American Cinderella Tale* by Robert D. San Souci

A Frog Prince by Alix Berenzy and *The Frog Prince, Continued* by Jon Scieszka

Little Red Riding Hood by Trina Schart Hyman and *Lon Po Po* by Ed Young

The Midas Touch by Jan Mark and *The Chocolate Touch* by Patrick Skene Catling

Oom Razoom by Diane Wolkstein and *I-Know-Not-What, I-Know-Not-Where* by Eric A. Kimmel

Told Two Ways

Individual Book Report Form

I read two versions of the same folk tale.

① Title:	② Title:
Author:	Author:

Compare them on this Venn diagram.

① ②

Write a paragraph that summarizes the similarities.

Figures of Speech

Individual Book Report Form

Literature Skill Focus: Identifying figurative language

1. Teaching the Literature Skill

- Introduce or review the terms *simile, metaphor,* and *personification.* A simile is a figure of speech that compares two things using the words *like* or *as.* A metaphor also compares two things, but the comparison is direct, without using *like* or *as.* Personification is when a thing or an animal is given human characteristics.

- Read pages 1 through 3 of *The Music of Dolphins* by Karen Hesse. This is the story of Mila, who has been raised by dolphins. After she is rescued, Mila learns human language and music in a laboratory. This book's text is rich with figurative language.

- Ask students to identify examples of similes, metaphors, and personification. For example, a metaphor is on page 1: "We laugh and laugh, riding the misty lid of the sea, bright beads of dolphin noise...." On page 2 is a simile: "It beats like a giant heart." On page 3 is an example of personification: "The moon paints a stripe of light."

2. Reading Independently

- Students choose a fiction book from the library. They take the book home to read independently. The students complete the form on page 27 and return it to school.

3. Sharing the Book Reports

- When the book reports have been returned, display them, have a class discussion about the literature skill in the students' books, or have partners share their books.

Good Books to Read

The Book of Three by Lloyd Alexander

Harlem: A Poem by Walter Dean Myers

Holes by Louis Sachar

Mrs. Frisby and the Rats of NIMH by Robert C. O'Brien

The Music of Dolphins by Karen Hesse

The Night Before Christmas by Clement C. Moore

Owl Moon by Jane Yolen

The Whipping Boy by Sid Fleischman

The Wind in the Willows by Kenneth Grahame

I am a writer. I always use figurative language!

Name_____

Figures of Speech
Individual Book Report Form

Title:

Author: | Page Count:

As you read, record examples of similes, metaphors, and personification.

Similes "It beats like a giant heart."

Metaphors "...bright beads of dolphin noise."

Personification "The moon paints a stripe of light."

It Happened to Me, Too!
Individual Book Report Form

Literature Skill Focus: Comparing personal experiences to realistic fiction

1. Teaching the Literature Skill

- Briefly review the genre of *realistic fiction*. In realistic fiction, the characters, settings, and details seem real, and they are based on events that could really happen.

- Read chapter 1 of *Bridge to Terabithia* by Katherine Paterson. This chapter introduces Jess and his family and reveals Jess's dream to become the fastest runner in his fifth-grade class. Ask students if the chapter seemed realistic. Have them think of experiences in their lives that are similar to those in the chapter.

2. Reading Independently

- Have students choose a realistic fiction book from the library. They take the book home to read independently. The students complete the form on page 29 and return it to school.

3. Sharing the Book Reports

- When the book reports have been returned, display them, have a class discussion about the literature skill in the students' books, or have partners share their books.

Good Books to Read

The Best Christmas Pageant Ever by Barbara Robinson

Bridge to Terabithia by Katherine Paterson

Dear Mr. Henshaw by Beverly Cleary

Harriet the Spy by Louise Fitzhugh

Maniac Magee by Jerry Spinelli

The Missing 'Gator of Gumbo Limbo by Jean Craighead George

Starring Sally J. Freedman as Herself by Judy Blume

Thank You, Mr. Falker by Patricia Polacco

The Toilet Paper Tigers by Gordan Korman

I know just how that guy felt!

How to Report on Books • EMC 6010 • © Evan-Moor Corp

It Happened to Me, Too!
Individual Book Report Form

Title:	
Author:	Page Count:

Think about something in the story that is similar to something that has happened to you in your own life.

_____
character's name

_____
place

_____
time

Write about it.

_____
my name

_____
place

_____
time

Write about it.

You, the Reader

Individual Book Report Form

Literature Skill Focus: Evaluating your reading habits

1. Teaching the Literature Skill

- As students become independent readers, they should evaluate the reasons they choose to read books.

- Brainstorm with students some reasons why they choose to read. Some possible responses might include favorite author, interesting topic, appealing book jacket, recommendation from a friend, required reading by teacher.

- Explain that for this book report students will complete a survey that may help them learn about themselves as readers.

2. Reading Independently

- Students choose a book from the library. They take the book home to read independently. The students complete the form on page 31 and return it to school.

3. Sharing the Book Reports

- When the book reports have been returned, display them, have a class discussion about the literature skill in the students' books, or have partners share their books.

Good Books to Read

Among the Hidden by Margaret Peterson Haddix

Homeless Bird by Gloria Whelan

The Hundred Dresses by Eleanor Estes

The Kite Rider by Geraldine McCaughrean

Pictures of Hollis Woods by Patricia Reilly Giff

The Skin I'm In by Sharon G. Flake

Song of the Trees by Mildred D. Taylor

Thin Wood Walls by David Patneaude

Walt Whitman: Words for America by Barbara Kerley

Year of Impossible Goodbyes by Sook Nyul Choi

I prefer a good mystery!

Name_____

You, the Reader
Individual Book Report Form

1. What words pop into your mind when you think of reading a book?
_____

2. How many minutes a day do you read at home? _____ minutes

3. Where's your favorite place to read at home?
_____

4. How do you find books you love to read?
_____

_____

5. Besides books, what other materials do you read?
_____

6. Do you have a library card?   yes   no

   How many times a month do you visit the library

   to check out books? _____ times

7. My favorite author is _____.

8. The best book I've read is _____.

9. The best book someone read to me is _____.

10. The kinds of books I enjoy reading are _____.

11. I watch TV for _____ hours a day because _____

_____.

12. I have read a book longer than 100 pages.   yes   no

13. What did you learn about yourself as a reader?
_____

_____

_____

My Recommendation
Individual Book Report Form

Literature Skill Focus: Recommending a book

1. Teaching the Literature Skill
- As a class, brainstorm the components of a good book recommendation. For example, a good recommendation:

  tells a little, but not too much about the book;

  gives the correct author and title so the book is easy to find; and

  gives enough details about the story so that the recommendation is valuable.

- Read chapter 1 of *When Zachary Beaver Came to Town* by Kimberly Willis Holt. Model how to write a recommendation for a friend. For example, This book is interesting right away. The characters remind me of my friends at school. The kid who is telling the story is kind of shy. Some of the things he observes about people are very funny.

2. Reading Independently
- Have students choose a book from the library. They take the book home to read independently. The students complete the form on page 33 and return it to school.

3. Sharing the Book Reports
- When the book reports have been returned, display them, have a class discussion about the literature skill in the students' books, or have partners share their books.

Good Books to Read

The Bad Beginning by Lemony Snicket

Bud, Not Buddy by Christopher Paul Curtis

Esperanza Rising by Pam Muñoz Ryan

Hatchet by Gary Paulsen

Holes by Louis Sachar

Shiloh by Phyllis Reynolds Naylor

The Summer of the Swans by Betsy Byars

The Teacher's Funeral: A Comedy in Three Parts by Richard Peck

The Trumpet of the Swan by E. B. White

Volcanoes by Seymour Simon

When Zachary Beaver Came to Town by Kimberly Willis Holt

Name_____

My Recommendation
Individual Book Report Form

Title:

Author: Page Count:

Who would like this book?

_____

_____

_____

Great Book!

What are some specific examples of things that make this a good book?

On a scale of 1 to 10, how would you rate this book?

1	2	3	4	5	6	7	8	9	10

Poor   Disappointing   Average   Good   Super

Parent Letter
Support Independent Reading

Dear Parent,

Even though your child has been reading independently for some time, you are still important to supporting his or her love of reading. There are several ways you can do this. Ask your child to tell you about the books he or she has checked out of the school library. Ask how well he or she is enjoying the books. Your child will be asked to do a report, an individual project, or a group project on a book. Share a book with your child by reading aloud to each other. Discuss the characters and the plot.

Savor this time together. You are the most influential person in your child's life.

Sincerely,

Dear Parent,

Even though your child has been reading independently for some time, you are still important to supporting his or her love of reading. There are several ways you can do this. Ask your child to tell you about the books he or she has checked out of the school library. Ask how well he or she is enjoying the books. Your child will be asked to do a report, an individual project, or a group project on a book. Share a book with your child by reading aloud to each other. Discuss the characters and the plot.

Savor this time together. You are the most influential person in your child's life.

Sincerely,

Individual Book Report Projects

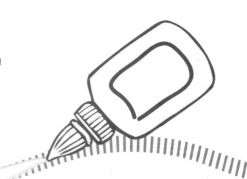

A Letter to a Character

Individual Book Report Project

Literature Skill Focus: Understanding a character

1. Teaching the Literature Skill

• Remind students that they get to know characters from reading about them. In their reading, they learn details about the characters' lives and what is important to the characters.

• Read chapter I of *Ella Enchanted* by Gail Carson Levine. Brainstorm what students learned about the main character in this chapter. Record their ideas. Ask students what questions they would like to ask the main character.

• Using the information from the discussion, model how to write a friendly letter to the main character.

2. Modeling the Book Project

• Explain to students that they will read a book independently and write a friendly letter to the main character.

• Have students brainstorm symbols and colors to include in a border for a letter to Ella.

• Show students how to make the envelope for their letter.

3. Reading Independently

• Have students choose a fiction book from the library. They take the book home to read independently. Students complete the book report projects and return them to school.

4. Sharing the Book Projects

• When the projects have been returned, set up a display and allow students to share their work. The time invested will encourage other students to read new books.

How to Make the Envelope for a Letter to a Character

I. Choose a character. Think about what you have learned about this character from reading the book. Think of some questions you would like to ask the character.

2. Write a friendly letter to the character. Draw a border the character would like.

3. Make the envelope on page 37. Decorate it to match your letter. Fold your letter and place it in the envelope.

Dear Ella,
Why was your story called *Ella Enchanted*? I think I know why, but I would like to hear your side.
Sincerely,
Samantha

March 25, 2006

To: Ella of Frell
Kingdom of Kyrria

A Letter to a Character
Individual Book Report Project

1. Write a friendly letter to a character.
2. Decorate the border of your letter with words, pictures, and colors that represent your character.
3. Make the envelope below. Decorate it to match the letter. Fill in the information on the envelope.
4. Fold the letter and place it inside.

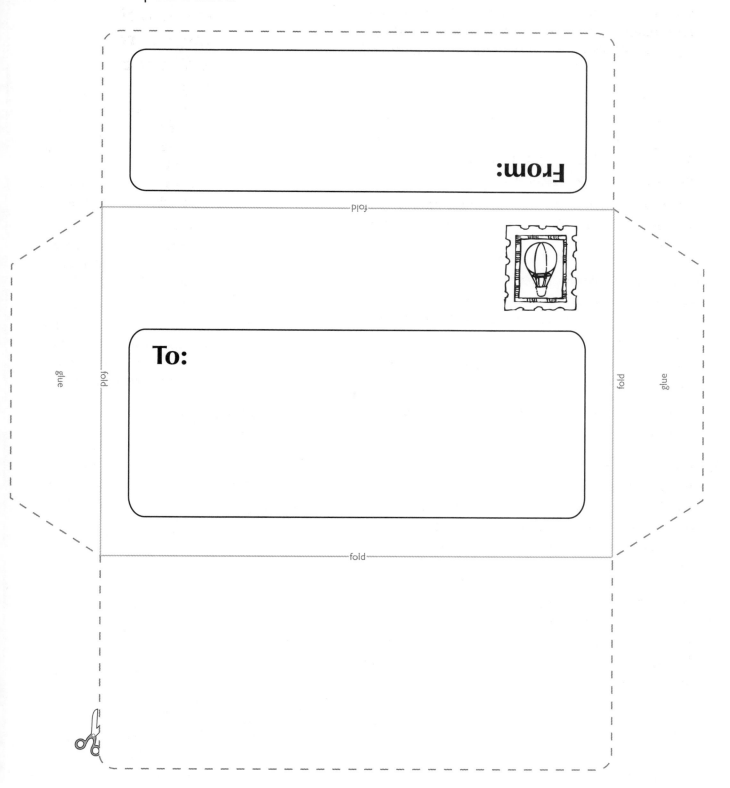

From:

To:

fold

fold

fold

fold

glue

glue

Showing the Setting
Individual Book Report Project

Literature Skill Focus: Identifying the setting and representing it on a poster

1. Teaching the Literature Skill

- Review with students the elements of the setting of a story. The setting includes both the place and the time in which the story happens.

- Read the beginning pages of *Belle Prater's Boy* by Ruth White. Ask students to listen for clues to the setting.

- Ask students to share their clues to the setting. Record them on a transparency copy of the chart on page 39. The setting is Coal Station, Virginia, a small town in the Appalachian Mountains, early in the spring of 1954.

2. Modeling the Book Project

- Before the lesson, gather some pictures that represent the setting, such as a map of Virginia, or pictures of the Appalachian Mountains, coal mines, flowering trees, etc. Locate Coal Station on the map of Virginia and mark it.

- Arrange the pictures. Add a heading that tells the time and place.

- If there is room, add drawings of characters engaged in some activity from the plot.

3. Reading Independently

- Have students choose a fiction book from the library. They take the book home to read independently. Using the chart, the students make setting posters. They return the books and the posters to school.

4. Sharing the Book Projects

- When the book projects have been returned, set up a display and allow time for students to share their work. The time spent will encourage other students to read new books.

How to Make a Setting Poster

1. Reread the setting descriptions in the story. On the chart on page 39, note the geographic location, the time of year, and other clues to where and when the story takes place.

2. Find maps or pictures of landforms or seasons, etc., to put on your poster.

3. On a 12" x 18" (30.5 x 45.5 cm) sheet of construction paper, arrange the maps and pictures. Glue them in place.

4. Add a headline that tells the time and place in which the story is set.

5. Write captions for the pictures.

6. Glue the chart onto the back of the poster.

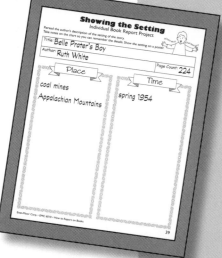

Showing the Setting
Individual Book Report Project

Reread the author's description of the setting of the story.
Take notes on the chart so you can remember the details. Show the setting on a poster.
Write your name on the back of the poster.

Where am I?   What time is it?

Title:

Author: Page Count:

Place

Time

Just Give Me the Facts

Individual Book Report Project

Literature Skill Focus: Recognizing facts in a fiction text

1. Teaching the Literature Skill

- Tell students that facts can be found in fiction books. The Thirteen Moons series of books by Jean Craighead George are great examples. Ms. George presents factual information about animals in the context of a fiction story.

- Read *The Moon of the Alligators*.

- Brainstorm facts found in the first two pages, such as an alligator's eyes are on the top and to the rear of its head. The Everglades of Florida is not a swamp, but a river. The Everglades is forty to sixty miles wide and a hundred miles long.

- Record the facts on a chart.

2. Modeling the Book Project

- Tell students that they will be writing five facts on five squares of paper and stapling them to the robot pattern on page 41.

3. Reading Independently

- Have students choose a fiction book from the library. They take the book home to read independently. The students make the projects and return them to school.

4. Sharing the Book Projects

- When the book projects have been returned, set up a display and allow time for students to share their work. The time will be well spent because it will encourage other students to read new books.

How to Make the Project

1. Copy five facts you have discovered on five 3" x 3" (7.5 cm) squares of paper.

2. Fill in the book information on the robot form.

3. Staple the squares to the form as indicated.

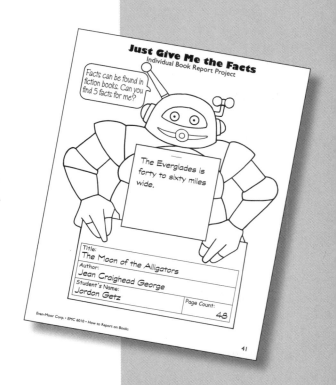

Just Give Me the Facts
Individual Book Report Project

Facts can be found in fiction books. Can you find 5 facts for me?

Staple facts here.

Title:

Author:

Student's Name:

Page Count:

Theme Chart
Individual Book Report Project

Literature Skill Focus: Identifying the theme of a book

1. Teaching the Literature Skill

- Briefly review the term *theme*. The theme of a story is a message about life that the writer shares with the reader. Often the reader must figure out the theme because it is not actually stated. Like a good detective, the reader gathers evidence from the story that points to the theme.

- Discuss with students a book you have read together. *Rodzina* by Karen Cushman is a good example. It's a story about a Polish girl's journey from Chicago to the West on an orphan train in 1881. Have students retell the story and then think of a theme that Karen Cushman is sharing with the reader. For example, there is hope in what seems like a hopeless situation.

2. Modeling the Book Project

- Brainstorm the clues to the theme you discovered in *Rodzina*. Write the clues on a chart or a transparency copy of the form on page 43.

3. Reading Independently

- Have students choose a book from the library. They take the book home to read independently. The students complete the theme charts. They return the books and the charts to school.

4. Sharing the Book Projects

- When the book projects have been returned, set up a display and allow time for students to share their work. The time will be well spent because it will encourage other students to read new books.

How to Make the Theme Chart

1. Fill in the book information.

2. As you read, take notes on the clues the author gives you about the theme.

3. Write the theme of the book on the chart.

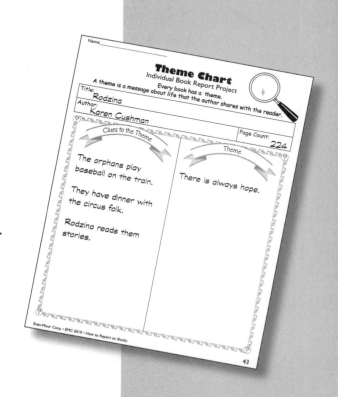

Theme Chart
Individual Book Report Project
Every book has a theme.
A theme is a message about life that the author shares with the reader.

Title:

Author:

Page Count:

Clues to the Theme

Theme

Conflicting Goals
Individual Book Report Project

Literature Skill Focus: Identifying the conflict in a story

1. Teaching the Literature Skill

- Introduce or review the term *conflict*. A conflict is a struggle between two characters or forces in a story. There are several different types of conflicts: person against person, person against self, person against society, person against nature, or person against fate or God.

- Read *Mufaro's Beautiful Daughters* by John Steptoe. Ask students to listen for the differences between the two characters, Nyasha and Manyara.

2. Modeling the Book Project

- On a chart or a transparency copy of page 45, brainstorm with students the problems faced by the two characters, their goals, and the action each took toward her goal. Then add the solution to each character's problem.

3. Reading Independently

- Have students choose a fiction book from the library. They take the book home to read independently. Students identify the conflict in the book and complete the chart on page 45. They return the books and the charts to school.

4. Sharing the Book Projects

- When the book projects have been returned, set up a display and allow time for students to share their work. The time will be well spent because students will be encouraged to read new books.

How to Make a Conflicting Goals Book Project

1. Decide on the two characters who have conflicting goals. Write their names on the chart.

2. Write down the problems faced by the two characters.

3. Decide on the goal of each character.

4. Summarize the action taken by each character toward his or her goal.

5. Write down the solution to each character's problem.

How to Report on Books • EMC 6010 • © Evan-Moor Cor

Conflicting Goals
Individual Book Report Project

A conflict is a struggle between two characters or forces in a story.

Title: _____

Author: _____ Page Count: _____

Student's Name: _____

Character:	Character:
Problem:	Problem:
Goal:	Goal:
Action:	Action:
Solution:	Solution:

ID the Character

Individual Book Report Project

Literature Skill Focus: Recalling details about the main character

1. Teaching the Literature Skill
- Read chapter I of *Number the Stars* by Lois Lowry. Have students identify the main characters, Ellen and Annemarie. Brainstorm and record details about one character. For example, Annemarie Johansen loves to run. She is a good student. She is ten years old and has long legs and silvery blond hair. Annemarie is Danish.

2. Modeling the Book Project
- Model how to make an ID card for the character you discussed in the lesson.

3. Reading Independently
- Have students choose a fiction book from the library. They take the book home to read independently.

- Students make character ID cards for the main character of their book and return the books and the ID cards to school.

4. Sharing the Book Projects
- When the book projects have been returned, set up a display and allow time for students to share their work.

How to Make a Character ID Card

1. Fill in the information on both sides of the card.

2. Draw a picture or cut an illustration from a magazine that matches the physical description of the character.

3. Cut out the patterns. Glue them onto the front and back of a 5½" x 8½" (14 x 21.5 cm) piece of construction paper.

4. Punch a hole as indicated and thread a 24" (61 cm) piece of string through the hole. Tie the loose ends together.

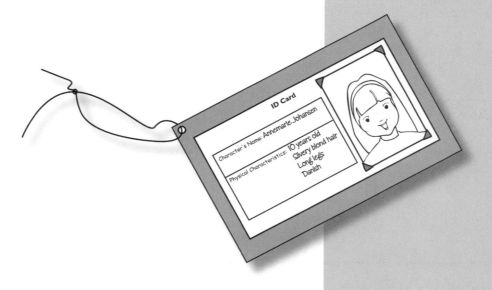

ID the Character
Individual Book Report Project

in the information on both sides of the character ID card.
e the main character from your book. Write your name on the bottom of the card.

Character ID Card

Character's Name:

Physical Characteristics:

Best Quality—What is the character's most admirable quality?

Goal—What does the character want to do or be?

A Character Diary

Individual Book Report Project

Literature Skill Focus: Retelling events from one character's point of view

1. Teaching the Literature Skill

- Review the term *point of view*. Remind students that sometimes stories are written from a character's point of view and sometimes from the point of view of someone outside the story.

- Read chapter one of *The Cricket in Times Square* by George Selden. Ask students to identify the point of view. The story is told by someone outside the story.

- Model how to write a diary entry from the point of view of Tucker Mouse, one of the characters. For example, Saturday night, Grand Central Station. Poor Mario. No one wants to buy his papers. Paul the conductor bought one and he didn't even wait for his change. Paul wanted Mario to have the extra money. I like Paul. I've got to get to bed. But what's that strange sound?

2. Modeling the Book Project

- Explain to students that they are to write from a point of view that is different from the one in their book. Encourage students to add details such as dates and places to make their diary entries more authentic.

3. Reading Independently

- Have students choose a fiction book from the library. They take the book home to read independently. Students make a diary and write three entries from a different point of view than the one in the book.

4. Sharing the Book Projects

- When the book projects have been returned, set up a display and allow time for students to share their work.

How to Make a Diary

1. Fold a piece of 6" x 18" (15 x 45.5 cm) paper as shown.

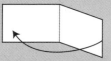

2. Fill in the information on the form on page 49.

3. Cut out the form and glue it to the accordion book.

4. Write the date and an entry on each of the remaining pages of the book. Add drawings and color.

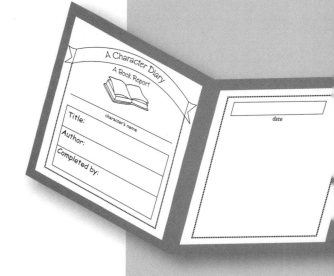

A Character Diary
Individual Book Report Project

me the role of a character from your book.
te three diary entries for the character.

A Character Diary
A Book Report

character's name

Title:

Author:

Completed by:

date

date

date

My Bookmark

Individual Book Report Project

Literature Skill Focus: Identifying story elements

1. Teaching the Literature Skill

• Read a picture book such as *Fly Away Home* by Eve Bunting to your class.

• Review with students the basic story elements, including characters, setting, problem, events, and solution.

2. Modeling the Book Project

• On a chart or a transparency copy of the form on page 51, brainstorm the story elements for *Fly Away Home*.

• Discuss ways to decorate the bookmark using images from the story.

3. Reading Independently

• Have students choose a fiction book from the library. They take the book home to read independently. Students return their bookmarks and their books to school.

4. Sharing the Book Projects

• When the book projects have been returned, set up a display and allow time for students to share their work.

How to Make a Story Elements Bookmark

1. Complete the story information on the bookmark form.

2. Decorate the bookmark with images from the story.

3. Fold the bookmark along the center fold line and glue or tape the edges together.

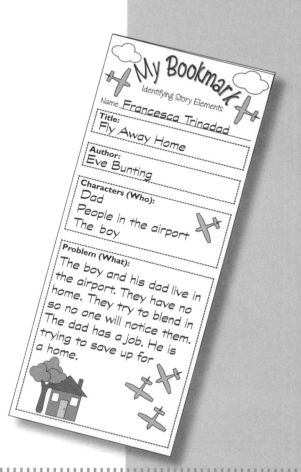

My Bookmark
Individual Book Report Project

My Bookmark
Identifying Story Elements

Name _____

Title:

Author:

Characters (Who):

Problem (What):

fold

Events (What Happened):

Solution (How):

How would you rate this book?

A Book Interview
Individual Book Report Project

Literature Skill Focus: Recalling story details

1. Teaching the Literature Skill

- Ask students to describe an interview. In an interview, the interviewer asks questions. The person being interviewed, usually an expert on a specific subject, answers the questions. Interviews are one way to learn about something or someone.

- Explain to students that when they finish reading their books, they will be experts on those books. They will be interviewed by a classmate so the classmate can learn about the book they read.

2. Modeling the Book Project

- Read a Caldecott Medal-winning book, such as *Lon Po Po* by Ed Young, to your class. This is a Red Riding Hood story from China.

- Ask a student to interview you using the questions on page 53.

3. Reading Independently

- Have students choose a Caldecott Medal-winning book from the library. They take the book home to read independently. Students prepare for their interview by completing the form on page 53.

4. Sharing the Book Projects

- When students return the books to school, they will be interviewed by another student.

How to Do a Book Interview

1. Read a book carefully. Review the book to make sure that you remember the setting, characters, and plot of the story.

2. Write out the answers to the interview questions on the form on page 53.

3. Have students work in pairs and interview each other.

A Book Interview
Individual Book Report Project

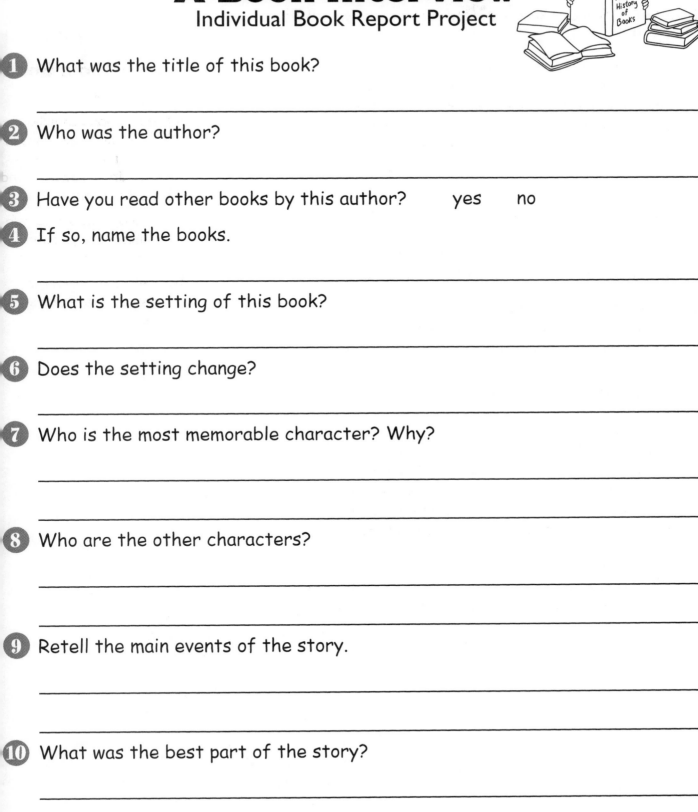

1 What was the title of this book?

_____

2 Who was the author?

_____

3 Have you read other books by this author?   yes   no

4 If so, name the books.

_____

5 What is the setting of this book?

_____

6 Does the setting change?

_____

7 Who is the most memorable character? Why?

_____

_____

8 Who are the other characters?

_____

_____

9 Retell the main events of the story.

_____

_____

10 What was the best part of the story?

_____

_____

Two Characters
Individual Book Report Project

Literature Skill Focus: Comparing and contrasting two characters

1. Teaching the Literature Skill

- Brainstorm with students the ways that authors reveal the traits of a character. For example, the physical description of the character, the observations of other characters, the words and actions of the character, etc.

- Ask students to write down key words that describe the traits of the two main characters as you read chapters 1 and 2 of *The Whipping Boy* by Sid Fleischman.

2. Modeling the Book Project

- As a class, brainstorm words and phrases that describe the personality traits of Jemmy and Prince Brat.

- Discuss the ways they are alike and the ways they are different.

3. Reading Independently

- Have students choose a fiction book from the library. They take the book home to read independently. Students complete the compare-and-contrast form for two characters in their book. They return the books and the forms to school.

4. Sharing the Book Projects

- When the book projects have been returned, set up a display and allow time for students to share their work.

How to Compare and Contrast Two Characters

1. Choose two interesting characters from the book you read.

2. Fill out the form on page 55 with the information you learned about the characters.

3. Think of some ways the two characters are alike and some ways they are different.

ame_____

Two Characters
Individual Book Report Project

This chart will help you describe the similarities and differences between two characters in the book you read.

Title:		
Author:		
Characters' names	1	2
Physical appearance		
Personality traits		
Actions and behavior		
Thoughts and feelings		
Relationships with others		
What the character wants		

How are the two characters alike?

_____

_____

How are the two characters different?

_____

_____

A Story Bag

Individual Book Report Project

Literature Skill Focus: Retelling a story with props

1. Teaching the Literature Skill
- Review with students the idea of retelling a story. Emphasize that it is important to highlight important events and characters, but not to tell every detail.
- Read *The Talking Eggs* by Robert D. San Souci or another picture book.
- Brainstorm a list of objects or symbols that could represent characters or events in the story. For example, a fan might represent Mama and Rose. A cup could represent Blanche's kindness to the old woman. A twig might stand for Blanche running away in the forest.

2. Modeling the Book Project
- Using the list of objects from the lesson, show students how to plan the retelling of the story. For example, the story begins by introducing Rose, Blanche, and the widow. This bean stands for all the work Mama makes Blanche do.

3. Reading Independently
- Have students choose a picture book from the library. They take the book home to read independently. Students gather objects to put in their story bags and practice retelling their stories. Then the students return their books and the story bags to school.

4. Sharing the Book Projects
- When the story bags are returned, set up a display and allow time for students to retell their stories. The time invested will encourage students to read as they practice their oral presentation skills.

How to Make a Story Bag

1. Fill out the bag label and glue it to a brown paper bag.
2. Brainstorm five to ten objects that symbolize an important event or represent a character in the story.
3. Put the objects in the bag.
4. Practice retelling the story, pulling the objects out of the bag as prompts.

A Story Bag
Title: The Talking Eggs
Author: Robert D. San Souci

jeweled eggs
fancy dress
shoes
carriage

Bag Prepared by *Oliver Caird*

56

A Story Bag
Individual Book Report Project

. Fill out the bag label. Glue it to a brown paper bag.
. Think of five to ten objects that represent events or characters in the story.
. Put the objects in the bag.
. Practice retelling the story using the objects as prompts.

A Story Bag

Title:

Author:

Summary:

Bag Prepared by _____

A Spiral Mobile
Individual Book Report Project

Literature Skill Focus: Recognizing foreshadowing

1. Teaching the Literature Skill
- Introduce the term *foreshadowing*. Foreshadowing is the technique of giving clues to coming events. An example of foreshadowing can be found on the first two pages of *Up a Road Slowly* by Irene Hunt.

- After you read these pages, ask students to identify clues that suggest what is going to happen next. For example, "I was still weak from the same sickness that had stricken my mother...." "I remembered quickly that it was not a day for laughter." "The smallest child asks, 'You're not going to live here anymore, are you?' "

2. Modeling the Book Project
- Using the clues from the lesson, demonstrate how to make the mobile.

3. Reading Independently
- Have students choose a fiction book from the library. They take the book home to read independently. Students make book report mobiles and return the books and the mobiles to school.

4. Sharing the Book Projects
- When the book projects have been returned, hang them from the ceiling and allow time for students to share their work. The time invested will encourage other students to read new books.

How to Make a Spiral Mobile

1. Fill in the information on the spiral pattern.
2. Glue the spiral shape on colored construction paper. Then cut out the spiral.
3. Punch a hole as indicated.
4. Make a loop of string or yarn to hang the mobile.

A Spiral Mobile
Individual Book Report Project

1. Fill in the information on the spiral.
2. Mount it on colored construction paper.
3. Cut it out, leaving a narrow border of color.
4. Punch a hole. Attach a piece of string to hang the spiral.

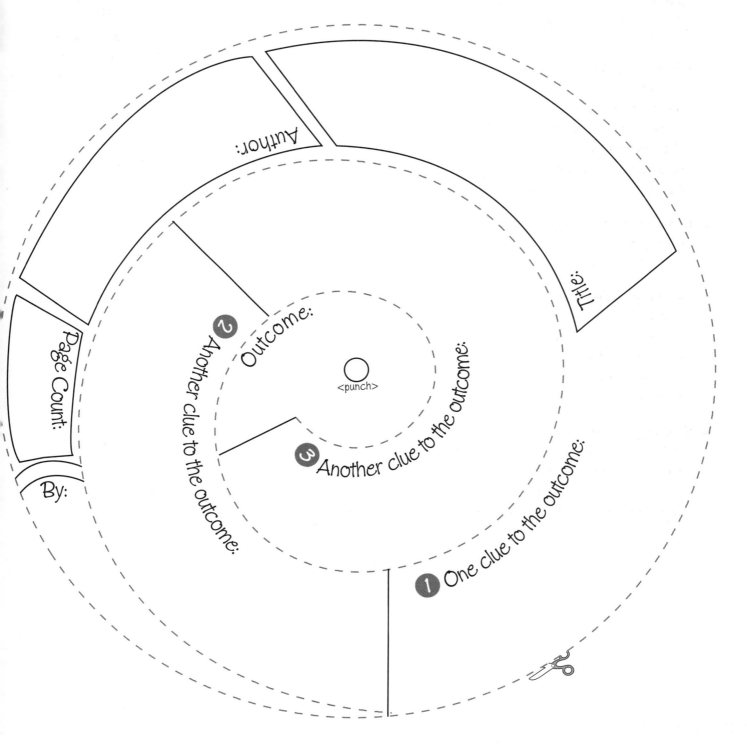

An Exciting Event Pop-up
Individual Book Report Project

Literature Skill Focus: Summarizing an exciting story event

1. Teaching the Literature Skill
- Ask students to brainstorm definitions for the word *exciting*. Write a class definition of the word.
- Read the first three pages of *Lyddie* by Katherine Paterson. Ask the class if the episode about the bear's visit to Lyddie's home fits the definition of *exciting*.
- Model how to write a summary of the exciting event. Emphasize that a summary tells the important action in a few sentences.

2. Modeling the Book Project
- As a class, brainstorm an image that would represent the exciting event you have discussed, such as the bear with the pot of oatmeal on its head.
- Draw the image. Glue the illustration to the pop-up tab. Show students how to make the pop-up folder.

3. Reading Independently
- Have students choose a fiction book from the library. They take the book home to read independently. Students make pop-up summaries of exciting events in the books and return the books and the summaries to school.

4. Sharing the Book Projects
- When the book projects have been returned, set up a display and allow time for students to share their work. The time invested will be well spent because students will be encouraging other students to read new books.

How to Make an Exciting Event Pop-up

1. Complete the form.
2. Cut out the form and fold to make a pop-up folder.

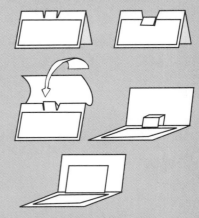

3. On a 3" x 5½" (7.5 x 14 cm) piece of construction paper, draw an image to show the exciting event.
4. Glue it to the pop-up tab.
5. Mount the pop-up folder onto a folded 8½" x 9" (21.5 x 23 cm) construction paper rectangle. Be careful not to glue the pop-up tab.

An Exciting Event Pop-up
Individual Book Report Project

An Exciting Event

fold

fold

glue

fold

An Exciting Story Event

_____

_____

_____

Title: _____

Author: _____

By: _____

The Hero

Individual Book Report Project

Literature Skill Focus: Defining a hero

1. Teaching the Literature Skill

- Initiate a class discussion about heroes. Have students brainstorm a list of heroes they have met in their reading. Discuss the common attributes of heroes. Ask questions to encourage them, such as, Do all heroes have to be strong and physically fit? Does a hero always win a prize or an award?

- Develop a class definition of a hero.

2. Modeling the Book Project

- Using a hero from a book the class has read, show the students how to fill out the hero nomination form. Then make a model of a hero's medal to be presented to the character.

3. Reading Independently

- Have students choose a fiction book from the library. They take the book home to read independently.

- Students nominate one of the characters in the book for a hero's award, fill out the hero's nomination form, and make a hero's medal. Then they return the books and the book projects to school.

4. Sharing the Book Projects

- When the book projects have been returned, set up a display and allow time for students to share their work. The time invested will be well spent because students will be encouraging other students to read new books.

How to Make a Hero's Medal

1. On yellow construction paper, trace around a glass or a coaster to make a circle. Cut out the circle to make a medal.

2. Decorate the medal with a phrase or words that describe the hero.

3. Add two ribbons to the bottom of the medal.

4. Glue it to the form.

Hero Nomination Form
Name: _____
Age: _____
In 25 words or less, explain why you think this character should be called a hero.
_____
_____
Title: _____
Author: _____
Page Count: _____
Completed by _____

Strong

The Hero
Individual Book Report Project

Hero Nomination Form

Name: _____

Age: _____

In 25 words or less, explain why you think this character should be called a hero.

_____

_____

_____

_____

Title: _____

Author: _____

Page Count: _____

Completed by _____

Glue Medal Here

A Character Bookmark

Individual Book Report Project

Literature Skill Focus: Creating a character sketch

1. Teaching the Literature Skill
- Brainstorm qualities that make a character likeable. Record students' ideas on a chart or chalkboard.
- Choose a book that your class has just completed or read chapter I of *Hoot* by Carl Hiaasen. Ask students to name their favorite characters and use the list of likeable qualities to rate the characters.

2. Modeling the Book Project
- Using the list from the lesson, demonstrate how to make the character bookmark.

3. Reading Independently
- Have students choose a fiction book from the library. They take the book home to read independently. Students make character bookmarks and return the books and the bookmarks to school.

4. Sharing the Book Projects
- When the book projects have been returned, set up a display and allow time for students to share their work. The time invested will be well spent because students will be encouraging other students to read new books.

How to Make a Character Bookmark

1. Draw a picture of your favorite character in the frame on one side of the bookmark.

2. Fill in the book information, a description of the character, and the reason why the character is your favorite.

3. Cut out the bookmark.

4. Fold the bookmark in half. Glue or tape the edges together.

My Favorite Book Character

By Ryan Lambert

A Character Bookmark
Individual Book Report Project

Why I Like This Character

Title:	
Author:	
Page Count:	

A Description of My Favorite Character:

Why I Like This Character:

My Favorite Book Character

By _____

A New Ending

Individual Book Report Project

Literature Skill Focus: Creating an alternate ending to a story

1. Teaching the Literature Skill

- Have students retell the ending of a book you have read together. For example, *Call It Courage* by Armstrong Sperry is a Newbery Medal-winning novel about how a young Polynesian boy overcomes his fear of the sea. At the end, the young boy, Mafatu, returns home to the lagoon fire to greet his father.

- Brainstorm different endings for the book. One ending might be that Mafatu was lost at sea. Another is that Mafatu might have been adopted by another tribe, or that he boarded a ship and sailed to a distant land.

2. Modeling the Book Project

- Using a chart or a transparency copy of the organizer on page 67 and the information from the lesson, show students how to complete the project.

3. Reading Independently

- Have students choose a fiction book from the library. They take the book home to read independently.

- Students complete the graphic organizers. They return the books and the organizers to school.

4. Sharing the Book Projects

- When the book projects have been returned, set up a display and allow time for students to share their work. The time invested will encourage students to read new books.

How to Complete the New Ending Organizer

1. Fill in the information on the organizer on page 67.

2. Think of another way for the story to end.

3. Support your new ending with several examples from the story.

A New Ending
Individual Book Report Project

Name

Title:

Author:

Page Count:

Characters:

Ending:

New Ending:

This ending could work because

How to Report on Books • EMC 6010 • © Evan-Moor Corp.

67

Name_____

A New Ending
Individual Book Report Project

Title: _____

Author: _____

Page Count: _____

□ □

Characters: _____

_____

_____

Ending		New Ending
_____	□	_____
_____	□	_____
_____	□	_____
_____	□	_____
_____	□	_____
_____	□	_____
_____	□	_____
_____	□	_____
_____	□	_____
_____	□	_____
_____	□	_____
_____	□	_____

□ □

This ending could work because _____

_____

_____

Words That Pop Off the Page

Individual Book Report Project

Literature Skill Focus: Identifying figurative language

1. Teaching the Literature Skill

- With your class, review the figurative language terms *simile, metaphor,* and *personification*. Similes and metaphors compare two things. Similes use the words *like* or *as* to compare the two directly. Metaphors compare two things indirectly by implying that they are the same. Personification is the technique of giving human qualities to an animal or an object.

- Read the first two chapters of *Chasing Redbird* by Sharon Creech to your class. Have students write down examples of similes, metaphors, and personification as they listen.

2. Modeling the Book Project

- Using a chart or a transparency copy of the form on page 69, record examples of each type of figurative language. "The two houses yoked together as one" and "as driven as a chicken-eating dog in a henhouse" are examples of similes. "Life is a bowl of spaghetti" is a metaphor. An example of personification is "the white oak's pores oozed sticky gum."

3. Reading Independently

- Have students choose a fiction book from the library. They take the book home to read independently. Students return the books and their copies of the form on page 69 to school.

4. Sharing the Book Projects

- When the book projects have been returned, set up a display and allow time for students to share their work. The time invested will encourage students to read new books.

How to Complete the Project

1. Write the book title, author, and page count where indicated.

2. As you read, write down the pages that have examples of similes, metaphors, and personification.

3. When you have finished the book, choose a few of your favorite examples of figurative language.

4. Write your favorite examples on the form.

68

Words That Pop Off the Page
Individual Book Report Project

Title:

Author: Page Count:

As you read, look for examples of similes, metaphors, and personification. Add them to the ones below.

Similes "as driven as a chicken-eating dog in a henhouse"

Metaphors "Life is a bowl of spaghetti."

Personification "the white oak's pores oozed sticky gum"

An Autobiography

Individual Book Report Project

Literature Skill Focus: Understanding autobiography

1. Teaching the Literature Skill

- Review with students the genres of biography and autobiography. Explain that a biography is the story of a person's life that is told by someone else. An autobiography is told by the person him- or herself.

- Read aloud part of an autobiography that describes an influential person in the author's life. *Hit a Grand Slam!* by Alex Rodriguez and *The Abracadabra Kid* by Sid Fleischman are good examples of autobiographies.

- As you read, ask students to listen for a person who had a big influence on the author.

2. Modeling the Book Project

- Brainstorm with students an important person in the author's life. Describe the person's appearance and personality, as well as his or her relationship to the author. Expand the discussion to include examples of how that person influenced the author's life.

- Tell students that they will be using the form on page 71 to plan a poster. They will focus on a person who influenced the author of their book.

3. Reading Independently

- Have students choose an autobiography from the library. They take the book home to read independently.

- Students return the books and their completed posters to school.

4. Sharing the Book Projects

- When the book projects have been returned, set up a display and allow time for students to share their work.

How to Make the Poster

1. Think of a person in the author's life who had a big influence on him or her.

2. Take notes about that person on the form on page 71.

3. Using your notes, write two paragraphs about that person. In the first paragraph, write a description of the person. Tell how they met, what he or she looks like, and what his or her personality is like.

4. In the second paragraph, tell how that person made a difference in the author's life.

5. On a 12" x 18" (30.5 x 45.5 cm) sheet of construction paper, create a poster. Include a picture of the author and the influential person and your two paragraphs.

6. Complete the form and glue it on your poster.

An Autobiography
Individual Book Report Project

Title:

Author: Page Count:

Poster Created by:

Influential Person

Describe the person.

Describe how the person influenced the author.

Good Readers...

- **Predict**

  Look at the title, subtitle, pictures; ask yourself what they mean.

- **Visualize**

  Make pictures of the words in your mind.

- **Pause/Summarize**

  Recall the details of what you have read.

- **Adjust Reading Rate**

  Read slower or faster depending on the difficulty of the words.

- **Reread**

  Go back and read over parts that don't make sense.

Good Readers...

- **Predict**

  Look at the title, subtitle, pictures; ask yourself what they mean.

- **Visualize**

  Make pictures of the words in your mind.

- **Pause/Summarize**

  Recall the details of what you have read.

- **Adjust Reading Rate**

  Read slower or faster depending on the difficulty of the words.

- **Reread**

  Go back and read over parts that don't make sense.

Group
Book Report
Projects

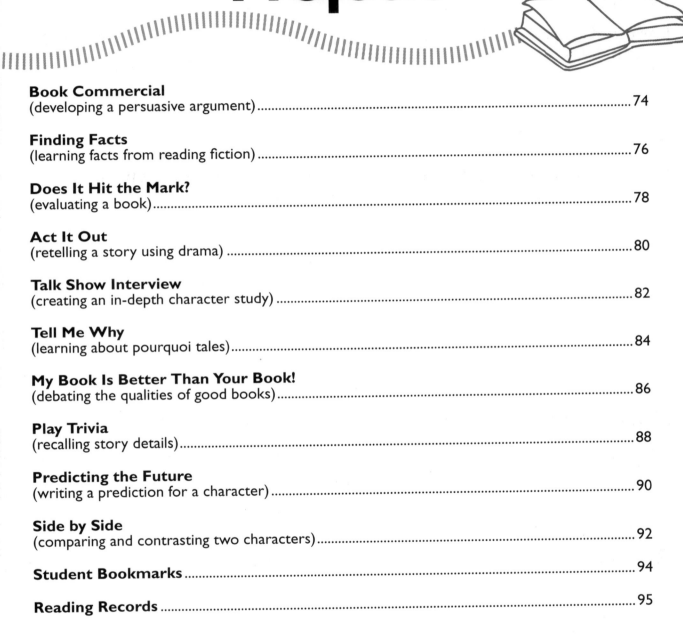

Book Commercial

Group Book Report Project

Literature Skill Focus: Developing a persuasive argument

1. Giving the Assignment

• As a class, brainstorm the attributes of a commercial message. Record students' ideas on a chart.

• Explain to students that they will be creating a commercial for the book that they read with their small groups. They will enact the finished commercial for the rest of the class.

2. Reading with a Small Group

• Assign students to work in small groups. Provide multiple copies of several different books. Assign a book title to each group. Each group member reads the book independently before the group work.

• Group members discuss the best "selling" points of the book. They fill out the commercial planning guide. Students plan and produce their commercial.

3. Sharing the Group Projects

• Invite each group to share its commercial with the class. If possible, videotape the performances. Leave the books in your classroom library so students can read the books that have been advertised.

How to Make a Commercial

1. Complete the planning guide on page 75.

2. Write a script. The script should tell who will talk and what will be said.

3. Rehearse the script and revise as needed.

4. Decide on props and costumes.

5. Rehearse the commercial until it's ready for presentation.

Awesome! Don't miss this one!

The BFG by Roald Dahl

The Whipping Boy by Sid Fleischman

THE GREAT BRAIN by John D. Fitzgerald

How to Report on Books • EMC 6010 • © Evan-Moor Cor

Book Commercial
Group Book Report Project

e this planning guide to organize the information you will use in your commercial.

Planning Guide

Title:

Author:

Summary of the Book:

Statement of Why Someone Would Want to Read the Book:

Slogan, Song, or Phrase to Be Repeated in Commercial:

Group Members:

Finding Facts
Group Book Report Project

Literature Skill Focus: Learning facts from reading fiction

1. Giving the Assignment

- Introduce or review the terms *realistic fiction* and *historical fiction*. Explain to students that sometimes a fictional story is based on real events or presents real information.

- Students will be reading realistic and historical fiction books and finding factual information. Each group will complete a research organizer that presents some of the facts the group has discovered.

2. Reading with a Small Group

- Assign students to work in small groups. Each group will read a historical or realistic fiction book. Provide multiple copies of several fiction books that include factual information. Assign each group a book. Each student reads the assigned book independently and completes a copy of the research organizer.

- In their groups, students discuss the factual information they learned by reading the book. On their copy of the research organizer, students write important facts they learned.

3. Sharing the Group Projects

- Invite each group to share its organizer with the class. When all groups have reported, ask students if they believe the books presented facts in an interesting way. Organizers may be displayed with the books to encourage other students to read them.

How to Complete the Research Organizer

1. Fill in the information on the research organizer on page 77.

2. Brainstorm the important facts from the book your group read.

3. Select five of the most important facts you learned. List them on the organizer.

Wow! I'm learning so many facts!

Finding Facts
Group Book Report Project

Research Organizer

Title: _____

Author: _____

Facts We Learned:

1. _____
   _____

2. _____
   _____

3. _____
   _____

4. _____
   _____

5. _____
   _____

Group Members:

Does It Hit the Mark?

Group Book Report Project

Literature Skill Focus: Evaluating a book

1. Giving the Assignment

- Brainstorm with students the qualities to consider when they evaluate a book. Direct the discussion toward story elements such as *interesting characters, good plot, realistic setting,* and *satisfying ending.* List the qualities on a chart or chalkboard for reference.

- On a chart or a transparency copy of page 79, complete the evaluation form for a book your class has read. Write a sentence to summarize each of the story elements.

- Explain that each group will evaluate the book they have read. They will present the results of the evaluation on a poster.

2. Reading with a Small Group

- Assign students to work in small groups. Assign each group a book. Each student independently reads the assigned book.

- In their groups, students use the evaluation form to rate the book they read. They create a poster to show if the book "hit the mark."

3. Sharing the Group Reports

- Invite each group to share its poster with the class.

How to Make a Hit the Mark Poster

1. Fill in the information on the evaluation form on page 79.

2. Write sentences to summarize each of the story elements.

3. Rate your book according to the quality of each element.

4. Mount your evaluation form on construction paper to make a poster.

I'll give it a 10!

Does It Hit the Mark?
Group Book Report Project

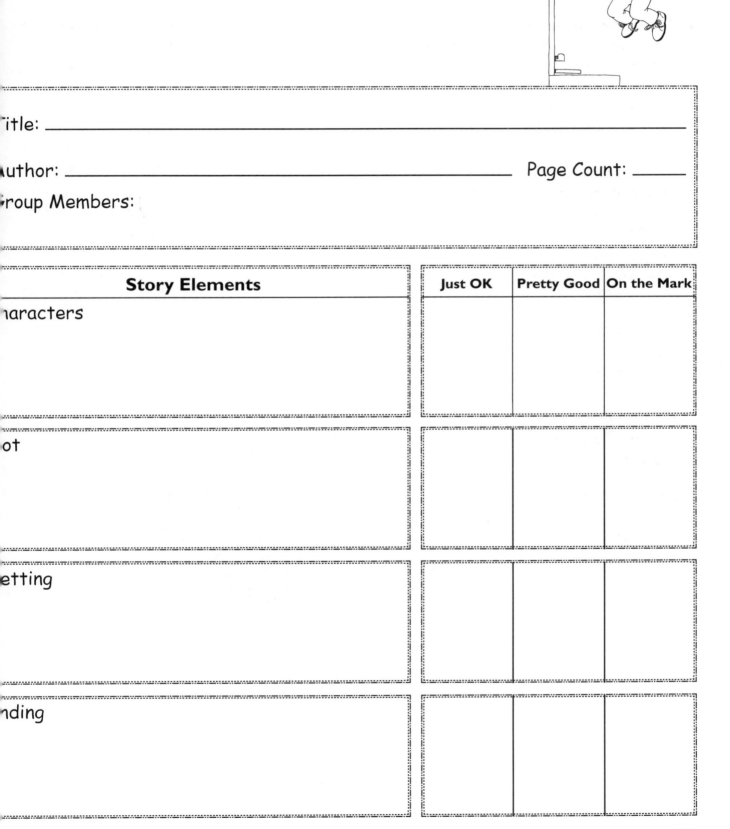

Title: _____

Author: _____ Page Count: _____

Group Members: _____

Story Elements	Just OK	Pretty Good	On the Mark
Characters			
Plot			
Setting			
Ending			

Act It Out
Group Book Report Project

Literature Skill Focus: Retelling a story using drama

1. Giving the Assignment

- Introduce to students the form of drama that uses a narrator to tell the story and individuals to act out the words.

- Using a folk tale such as *Anansi and the Spider* by Gerald McDermott, model how to create a storyboard to use as a script. For example, the narrator sets the scene by telling when and where the story takes place, as well as the beginning of the story. Group members will assume the roles of the characters and act out the events as the narrator tells the story. If there are any repeated words or phrases, these could be spoken by the whole group.

2. Reading with a Small Group

- Assign students to work in small groups. Assign each group a folk tale or fairy tale. Each student independently reads the assigned book.

- In their groups, students decide on the six most important events and create a storyboard. They choose a narrator and actors to act out the main events. Groups rehearse their plays and present them to the whole class.

3. Sharing the Group Projects

- Invite each group to act out their play for the class. Leave the books on display to encourage students to read new books.

How to Create a Story Board

1. Select six key events from your story. Draw or write these events on the storyboard form on page 81.

2. Decide on one person to be the narrator. Usually a narrator tells the story. Select actors for the story events.

3. Practice acting out the story so that it comes alive.

4. Present the play to the class.

In the time of the beginning of beginnings, everything and everyone lived on Ear...

How to Report on Books • EMC 6010 • © Evan-Moor C

Act It Out
Group Book Report Project

Title: _____

Author: _____ Narrator: _____

Other Actors: _____

_____

Storyboard

1	2	3
4	5	6

Talk Show Interview

Group Book Report Project

Literature Skill Focus: Creating an in-depth character study

1. Giving the Assignment

- Ask students if they have ever seen a talk show. Brainstorm the format of a talk show. A host asks guests questions and generally chats with them about what's happening in their lives.

- Explain to students that they will be posing as characters from a book and doing a talk show.

- Model how to write an introduction for a character. For example, for Emeralda in *The Frog Princess* by E. D. Baker: And now I'd like to introduce my next guest, Princess Emeralda. She is one princess who is not afraid to hold her ground. Today she's going to tell us about her adventure in the swamp with a frog.

2. Reading with a Small Group

- Assign students to work in small groups. Assign each group a book. Each student independently reads the assigned book.

- Using what they know about the book characters and their lives, students prepare and practice a talk show interview.

3. Sharing the Group Reports

- Invite groups to share their talk show interviews with the class. Display the interview forms with the books to encourage students to read new books.

How to Do a Talk Show Interview

1. From your book, choose three characters to be interviewed on the talk show.

2. Assign one person to be the talk show host and three others to be the guest characters.

3. As a group, write introductions for each of the characters.

4. Write questions for the host to ask all the guests.

5. Rehearse the talk show with the host introducing guests and asking the questions.

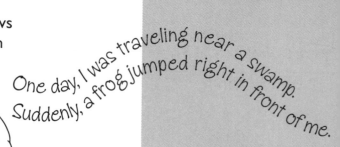

One day, I was traveling near a swamp. Suddenly, a frog jumped right in front of me.

Talk Show Interview
Group Book Report Project

ite an introduction and questions for each guest. Practice the talk show.

Title: _____

Author: _____ Page Count: _____

Guest 1 _____
character's name

Introduction:

Questions:

Guest 2 _____
character's name

Introduction:

Questions:

Guest 3 _____
character's name

Introduction:

Questions:

Group Members

Tell Me Why

Group Book Report Project

Literature Skill Focus: Learning about pourquoi tales

1. Giving the Assignment

- Review or introduce the genre of the *pourquoi (poor-kwa)* tale. *Pourquoi* is the French word for *why*. A pourquoi tale is a type of folk tale that explains the "why" of certain events, customs, or animal behaviors.

- Explain that in their groups, students will be looking for the attributes of pourquoi tales in the tales they read. Pourquoi tales explain how something in nature came to be; are about animal traits, nature, or people's customs; or feature animals or natural forces that have personalities and can speak. They often take place in the distant past and sound as if they are being told aloud.

2. Reading with a Small Group

- Assign students to work in small groups. Assign each group a pourquoi tale. Each student independently reads the assigned tale.

- As a group, students discuss their tale and decide what attributes of a pourquoi tale it contains.

- Each group records examples of each attribute on the form on page 85. They mount the form on construction paper to create a poster.

3. Sharing the Group Reports

- Display each poster. Invite each group to share their evaluations with the class. Display the books with the posters to encourage students to read new books.

How to Evaluate a Pourquoi Tale

1. Decide what question the tale asks.

2. Identify the main character and what form the character takes.

3. Identify the supporting characters.

4. Summarize the answer to the question.

5. Complete the form on page 85 by filling in the book information and the names of the group members.

Why do we have to share the sky?

How to Report on Books • EMC 6010 • © Evan-Moor C

Tell Me Why
Group Book Report Project

A pourquoi tale explains the "why" of certain events, customs, or animal behaviors.

Title: _____

Author: _____

This pourquoi tale asks...

Main Character:

Supporting Characters:

This tale answers the question this way:

Another way to answer the question is:

Group Members:

My Book Is Better Than Your Book!
Group Book Report Project

Literature Skill Focus: Debating the qualities of good books

1. Giving the Assignment

- Brainstorm with students the qualities that make a book really good to read. Some qualities might be the characters were just like my friends, the situations were so funny I laughed aloud, the plot kept me so interested I couldn't put the book down, etc.

- Tell students that they will be dividing their small groups into two teams and debating the qualities of the books they read. The purpose is to convince the whole class that their book is the best.

2. Reading with a Small Group

- Pick several books that are favorites with your students, or Newbery Medal-winning books. Assign students to work in small groups. Assign each group two books. Each group will form two teams. Each team member reads the assigned book.

- Team members discuss their books and complete the form on page 87.

3. Sharing the Group Reports

- Teams debate against each other to try to convince the other team that their book is better.

How to Prepare for the Debate

1. Brainstorm the qualities that make your book the best.

2. Write down examples of these qualities on the form on page 87.

3. Decide which quality makes your book better than the other teams' books.

The boy in this book survived a plane crash in the wilderness.

The main character in this book survived life in an orphanage.

Hatchet by Gary Paulsen

BUD, NOT BUDDY
BY CHRISTOPHER PAUL CURTIS

My Book Is Better Than Your Book!

Group Book Report Project

Title:

Author:

The best thing about this book is:

Here's an example:

Another great thing about this book is:

Here's an example:

The most outstanding feature of this book is:

Team Members:

Play Trivia

Group Book Report Project

Literature Skill Focus: Recalling story details

1. Giving the Assignment

- Ask students if they have ever played a trivia game. Discuss their experiences, and brainstorm the purposes of the game. One purpose is to recall facts about events and people. Ask them to imagine trivia questions about books.

- Model how to turn a trivia fact into a question. For example, in *Dear Mr. Henshaw* by Beverly Cleary, Leigh read Mr. Henshaw's book, *Ways to Amuse a Dog*. A question about that fact would be "What was the name of the book by Mr. Henshaw that Leigh read?"

2. Reading with a Small Group

- Assign students to work in small groups. Assign each group a book. Each student independently reads the assigned book.

- In their groups, students create a master list of 15 trivia questions and answers. Students copy the questions and answers onto index cards to create the trivia game.

- Groups can check their questions by playing the game and revising if necessary.

3. Sharing the Group Projects

- Create a pocket file folder for each trivia game. Display the trivia games with the books.

- As students read each book, have them play the trivia game and keep track of their scores.

How to Make a Trivia Game

1. Think of a trivia fact for the book your group read. Write the fact as a question on the master list on page 89. Write the answer and page number. Repeat for 15 questions.

2. Copy the trivia questions onto 3" x 5" (7.5 x 13 cm) index cards. Write the answers on the back of the cards. On the bottom right-hand corner of the card, write the name of the book and the number of the page where the answer can be found.

3. Check the questions and answers on the cards against the master list to make sure they match.

4. Play the game!

Play Trivia
Group Book Report Project

Write trivia questions and answers on this master list.
Copy the questions onto index cards. Write the page number where the answer can be found.

Title:

Author:

Group Members:

Questions	Answers	Page
1.		
2.		
3.		
4.		
5.		
6.		
7.		
8.		
9.		
10.		
11.		
12.		
13.		
14.		
15.		

Predicting the Future

Group Book Report Project

Literature Skill Focus: Writing a prediction for a character

1. Giving the Assignment

- Ask students if they have ever known someone so well that they could predict that person's future. Explain that this is possible with book characters as well as real people. For example, in *Dear Mr. Henshaw* by Beverly Cleary, we know that Leigh has the following personality traits: he is a writer, he is persistent, he is lonely, and he is inventive. Based on these traits, we could predict that Leigh will win a writing contest.

- Explain to students that they will be discussing a character in the books they read. They will decide on four personality traits that character shows. Based on those traits, they will write a prediction for that character's future.

2. Reading with a Small Group

- Assign students to work in small groups. Assign each group a book. Each student independently reads the assigned book.

- As a group, students complete the graphic organizer for the character they have chosen.

3. Sharing the Group Reports

- Invite each group to share its prediction with the class. Have students explain why each prediction fits the character's personality.

How to Predict a Character's Future

1. Decide which character you want to use from the book your group read.

2. Decide on four personality traits shown by that character in the book.

3. Based on those traits, predict one future action, career, or outcome for that character. Write this information on the form on page 91.

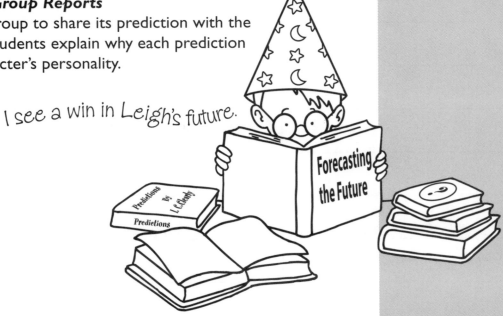

I see a win in Leigh's future.

How to Report on Books • EMC 6010 • © Evan-Moor Co

Predicting the Future
Group Book Report Project

Title:

Author:

Future Predicted for

_____
character

Trait	Trait	Trait	Trait

Prediction

Group Members:

Side by Side
Group Book Report Project

Literature Skill Focus: Comparing and contrasting two characters

1. Giving the Assignment
- Review the various ways a reader learns about characters. For example, the character's thoughts and words, the character's actions, the character's behavior toward other characters, and the words of the narrator all give information about individual characters.

- Discuss how to write a good comparison. Remind students that a comparison points out how two things are alike and how they are different. Introduce or review how to use a Venn diagram as a way to organize similarities and differences.

2. Reading with a Small Group
- Assign students to work in small groups. Assign each group a book. Each student independently reads the assigned book.

- Students choose two characters in the book and complete the Venn diagram on page 93. Then they write a comparison of the two characters.

3. Sharing the Group Reports
- Invite each group to share its comparison with the class. Display the posters in the classroom library area.

How to Compare and Contrast Two Characters

1. Choose two characters from the book your group read. Complete the Venn diagram on page 93.

2. On lined paper, write one paragraph that tells the ways the characters are the same. Then write another paragraph that tells how the characters are different.

3. Mount the Venn diagram form on construction paper to make a poster.

4. Glue your paper with the two paragraphs onto the back of the poster.

Let's see. They're both cupcakes. One has lots of frosting and the other has a cherry on top. ? ? ? ?

Side by Side
Group Book Report Project

Compare and contrast two characters.

| Title: |
| Author: |
| Group Members: |

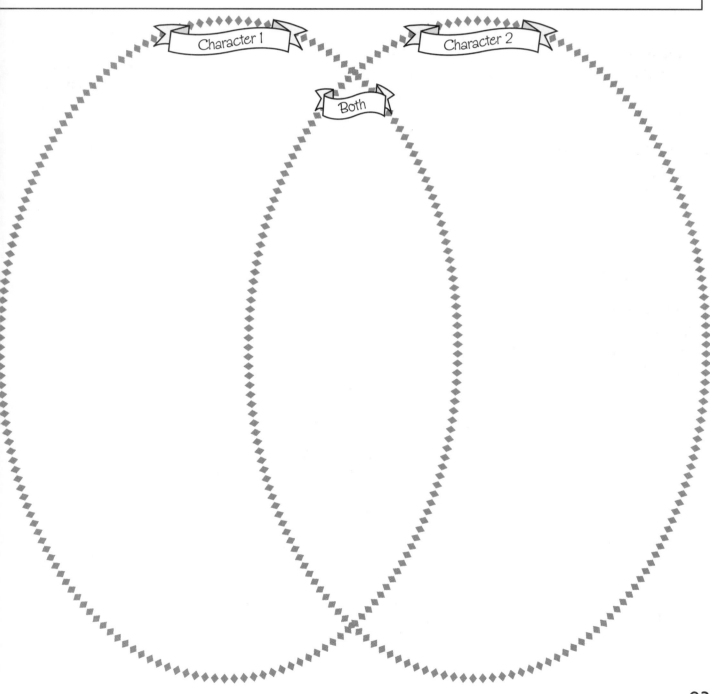

Character 1

Character 2

Both

Student Bookmarks

Guidelines for Group Book Report Projects

• Read the book assigned to your group.

• Use indoor voices.

• Respect everyone's ideas.

• One person talks at a time.

• Create a wonderful project.

Have fun!

Guidelines for Group Book Report Projects

• Read the book assigned to your group.

• Use indoor voices.

• Respect everyone's ideas.

• One person talks at a time.

• Create a wonderful project.

Have fun!

How to Report on Books • EMC 6010 • © Evan-Moor Corp.

Name_____

Reading Record

Use this to record the books that you read.

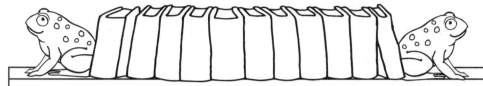

Date	Title	Author	Comments

Name_____

Reading Record

Use this to record the books that you read.

Date	Title	Author	Comments

How to Report on Books • EMC 6010 • © Evan-Moor Corp.